GAIN CONTROL OVER YOUR EMOTIONS

STOP ACTING RICH AND START GETTING RICH

BY

JAMES AMUCHE WHITNEY

Table of contents

Chapter 1

THE CONCEPT OF EMOTION

What Are Emotions?

How we interpret and respond to the world around us makes up who we are and contributes to our quality of life. The study of emotional psychology allows researchers to dive into what makes humans react as they do to certain stimuli and how those reactions affect us both physically and mentally. While the study of emotional psychology is vast and complex, only quite a bit about what constitutes our emotions and our behavioral and physical reactions to them has been discovered.

Emotions are often confused with feelings and mood, but the three terms are not interchangeable. According to the American Psychological Association (APA), emotion is defined as "a complex reaction pattern, involving experiential, behavioral and physiological elements." Emotions are how individuals deal with matters or situations they find personally significant. Emotional experiences have three components: a subjective experience, a physiological response, and a behavioral or expressive response.

Feelings arise from an emotional experience. Because a person is conscious of the experience, this is classified in the same category as hunger or pain. A feeling is the result of an emotion and may be influenced by memories, beliefs, and other factors.

A mood is described by the APA as “any short-lived emotional state, usually of low intensity.” Moods differ from emotions because they lack stimuli and have no clear starting point. For example, insults can trigger the emotion of anger while an angry mood may arise without apparent cause.

Defining emotion is a task that is not yet complete. Many researchers are still proposing theories about what makes up our emotions, and existing theories are constantly being challenged. Still, there’s a good basis of knowledge to analyze when exploring the topic.

The Process Of Emotion

While there is debate about the sequence, there is general agreement that emotions, as mentioned earlier, are made up of three parts: subjective experiences, physiological responses, and behavioral responses. Let’s look at each of these parts in more detail.

Subjective Experiences

All emotions begin with a subjective experience, also referred to as a stimulus, but what does that mean? While basic emotions are expressed by all individuals regardless of culture or upbringing, the experience that produces them can be highly subjective.

Subjective experiences can range from something as simple as seeing color to something as major as losing a loved one or getting married. No matter how intense the experience is, it can provoke many emotions in a single individual, and the emotions each feel may be different. For example, one person may feel anger and regret at the loss of a loved one while another may experience intense sadness.

Physiological Responses

We all know how it feels to have our hearts beat fast with fear. This physiological response is the result of the autonomic nervous system's reaction to the emotion we're experiencing. The autonomic nervous system controls our involuntary bodily responses and regulates our fight-or-flight response. According to many psychologists, our physiological responses are likely how emotion helped us evolve and survive as humans throughout history.

Interestingly, studies have shown autonomic physiological responses are strongest when a person's facial expressions most closely resemble the expression of the emotion they're experiencing. In other words, facial expressions play an important role in responding accordingly to an emotion in a physical sense.

Behavioral Responses

The behavioral response aspect of the emotional response is the actual expression of the emotion. Behavioral responses can include a smile, a grimace, a laugh, or a sigh, along with many other reactions depending on societal norms and personality.

While plentiful research suggests that many facial expressions are universal, such as a frown to indicate sadness, sociocultural norms and individual upbringings play a role in our behavioral responses. For example, how love is expressed is different both from person to person and across cultures.

Behavioral responses are important to signal to others how we're feeling, but research shows that they're also vital to individuals' well-being. A study in the Journal of Abnormal Psychology found that while watching negative and positive emotional films, suppression of behavioral responses to emotion had physical effects on the participants. The effects included elevated heart rates. This suggests that expressing behavioral responses to stimuli, both positive and negative, is better for your overall health than holding those responses inside. Thus, there are benefits of smiling, laughing, and healthily expressing negative emotions.

The physiological and behavioral responses associated with emotions illustrate that emotion is much more than a mental state. Emotion affects our whole demeanor and our health. Furthermore, our ability to understand others' behavioral responses plays a huge role in our emotional intelligence, which will be discussed in more detail later.

Basic And Complex Emotions

In emotional psychology, emotions are split into two groups: *basic and complex.*

Basic emotions

Basic emotions are associated with recognizable facial expressions and tend to happen automatically. Charles Darwin was the first to suggest that emotion-induced facial expressions are universal. This suggestion was a centerpiece idea to his theory of evolution, implying that emotions and their expressions were biological and adaptive. Emotions have been observed in animals by researchers for several years, suggesting that they're pivotal to survival in other species as well. Basic emotions are likely to have played a role in our survival throughout human evolution, signaling to those around us to react accordingly.

Emotional psychologist Paul Ekman identified six basic emotions that could be interpreted through facial expressions. They included happiness, sadness, fear, anger, surprise, and disgust. He expanded the list in 1999 to also include embarrassment, excitement, contempt, shame, pride, satisfaction, and amusement, though those additions have not been widely adopted.

List Of The Six Basic Emotions

Sadness

Happiness

Fear

Anger

Surprise

Disgust

Complex Emotions

Complex emotions have differing appearances and may not be as easily recognizable, such as grief, jealousy, or regret. Complex emotions are defined as "any emotion that is an aggregate of two or more others." The APA uses the example of hate being a fusion of fear, anger, and disgust. Basic emotions, on the other hand, are unmixed and innate. Other complex emotions include love, embarrassment, envy, gratitude, guilt, pride, and worry, among many others.

Complex emotions vary greatly in how they appear on a person's face and don't have easily recognizable expressions. Grief looks quite different between cultures and individuals. Some complex emotions, such as jealousy, may have no accompanying facial expression at all.

Benefits Of Understanding Emotions

As discussed, emotions have helped humans evolve and survive. According to Ekman, who developed the wheel of emotion, "It would be very dangerous if we didn't have emotions. It would also be a very dull life. Because our emotions drive us — excitement, pleasure, even anger." That is why we must be able to understand emotions as they play such an important role in how we behave.

Ekman argues that emotions are fundamentally constructive. They are influenced by what is good for our species overall and what we learned during our upbringing. They guide our behavior in a way that should lead us to a positive outcome. However, emotions can become destructive if the emotions we've learned are the correct response no longer fit our situation, or if subconscious emotions cause reactions that we are unable to understand. Being in touch with your emotions and turning your understanding into action is called emotional awareness. Being able to do this with others as well is referred to as emotional intelligence.

Emotional intelligence is the ability to perceive, control and evaluate emotions. The term was first coined by researchers Peter Salovey and John D. Mayer and found popularity through Dan Goleman's 1996 book. They define it as the ability to recognize, understand and manage our own emotions as well as recognize, understand and influence those of others. The study of emotional intelligence has gained much popularity since the mid-1990s, with business professionals, relationship coaches, and more using the term to encourage others to improve their lives. Many researchers believe that emotional intelligence can be improved over time, while some argue that it's a trait we're born with or without.

There are personal and professional benefits to improving your emotional intelligence. In Forbes, Co-Chair of Nobel Peace prize-nominated campaign and New York Times best-selling author Chade-Meng Tan addressed the benefits of improving emotional intelligence. He pointed out that high emotional intelligence correlates with better work performance, makes people better leaders, and creates the conditions for personal happiness. He stated, "There are also compelling personal benefits, and the most basic of those occur in three categories: calmness and clarity of mind, resilience, and more satisfying relationships."

Emotional intelligence plays a role in overall success much like traditional intelligence. Some researchers argue that it plays a bigger role. In his 1995 book "Emotional Intelligence: Why It Can Matter More Than IQ," psychologist Daniel Goleman introduced the idea of an EQ. Much like an IQ, an EQ is a measurement of an individual's emotional intelligence aptitude. Goleman argues that EQ counts twice as much as IQ and technical skills combined when it comes to becoming successful.

Whether or not that is true is certainly debatable, but emotional intelligence has served humans well throughout our evolution and history. It played a role long before it was officially defined, and likely will for years to come.

The components of emotional intelligence include:

Appraising and expressing emotions in the self and others: Recognizing or expressing verbal or nonverbal cues about emotion

Regulating emotion in the self and others: Managing emotions so that all parties are motivated towards a positive outcome.

Using emotions in adaptive ways: Using emotion and the interpretation of emotions to result in positive outcomes.

Those who have emotional intelligence open themselves to positive and negative emotional experiences, identify the emotions and communicate those emotions appropriately. Emotionally intelligent people can use their understanding of their emotions and the emotions of others to move toward personal and social growth. Those with low emotional intelligence may be unable to understand and control their emotions or those of others. This could leave others feeling bad when they don't understand their emotions, feelings, or expressions.

A few facts about emotions

Bad Feelings Are Good for Your Well-Being

Experiencing negative emotions such as fear and anger is important for mental health and helps us positively evaluate our experiences. Someone who only experiences positive emotions runs the risk of becoming complacent and ignoring the issues that matter. Negative emotions are perfectly natural and it's important not to suppress them. It's all about balance!

Emotions Are In Fact Physical

As well as being a psychological phenomenon, emotions are also felt outside of the brain in the rest of the body, according to a study by a team of scientists from Finland. Certain parts of the body, especially the upper half, are heavily stimulated during emotions such as love, happiness, and pride, whereas depression and sadness are linked to numbness.

Emotions Are Contagious

Research has proven time and time again that people unconsciously mimic the emotional expressions of those around them. Whether being "infected" with a smile or picking up positive energy online, we humans just can't help ourselves from "catching" emotions from other people.

Forcing a Smile Can Make You Happy

If you adjust your facial expression to reflect a certain emotion, you will begin to feel that emotion, studies have found. When you are happy you smile, right? But it works the other way, too. If you want to make yourself happy, all you have to do is force your face into a smile for around 30 seconds and you will instantly feel happier. It's that simple.

The Way You Feel is Always Written on Your Face

When a person experiences a strong emotion but tries to conceal their feelings, they let out a micro-expression—a brief involuntary expression of emotion. Micro-expressions occur so fast that they are often not seen in real-time, but when recorded and analyzed in slow motion they can provide a fascinating insight into a person's true emotional state

Colors Influence How You Feel

Different colors can stir up certain emotions because of what we associate with these hues from nature. For example, blue is a very calming color and enhances relaxation because it's associated with the ocean, whereas yellow is considered a joyous, vibrant color due to its connection to the sun.

Smells have quite an effect on our emotions

Good smells tend to elate human emotions while bad smells on the other hand take almost no time to trigger negative emotion.

Finance Theories

Classical finance theory considers probabilities and outcomes as the key influences when making decisions. The standard practice is to assume emotionless decision-making with efficient analysis of tradeoffs between alternatives.

Behavioral finance, however, considers the influence emotions have on decision-making.

Classical and behavioral theories are complementary as opposed to conflict. We use a blend of both approaches when making decisions. Business decisions, often considered an entirely rational exercise, can be improved by understanding how emotions interact with other motivations to drive our choices and behavior – some of these emotions and their impacts are explored below.

Anticipatory emotions

Anticipatory emotions – emotions we experience in anticipation of a future event – can affect our decisions, as well as the speed at which we make them. Some research suggests that when we feel positive anticipatory emotions, we make decisions more quickly.

As an example, when offered the chance to invest in a project that is promoted as offering the potential for high returns, some people might feel hope and excitement in anticipation of making a profit. As a result, they might act quickly to invest without taking the time to research the project or whether this is a sound investment.

Conversely, some people might feel anxious or fearful at the thought of giving up an investment that they have held for a long time, though it no longer performs well. What if they sell off the investment, then it starts performing well again? As a result, they delay selling. In these cases, emotions override rational analysis and also affect the speed at which the decisions were made.

Visceral emotions

Visceral emotions are emotions that we feel very deeply and find difficult to control or ignore. They operate at the subconscious level, separate from cognition and thinking, and include fear, hope, and dread. As an example, think about the panic and fear you would feel if you were charged by a grizzly bear.

Visceral emotions can have a significant effect on decision-making behavior. They can cause people to act against their self-interest with full knowledge they are doing so, and they can override our cognition and thought processes.

Consider the "panic selling" that occurred in the stock market in 2008 and 2020, during which the fear of a market meltdown caused many people to sell at the "bottom" of the market and incur a significant loss.

Errors in judgment often occur because individuals typically underestimate the influence of visceral factors when assessing their past, current, and future behavior. For example, when a choice must be made, we typically underestimate the pain caused by prior similar choices. Therefore, we are more likely to choose a course of action similar to past decisions.

Projection bias and state of mind

Projection bias is a subconscious influence on decisions and relates to the role emotions have on decision making. Projection bias is a self-forecasting error, where we overestimate how much our future selves will share our current emotional state and beliefs.

This bias causes us to make short-sighted decisions since individuals disproportionately use their current emotional state to predict future states. For example, hungry shoppers buy relatively more, and make different selections, even though their future needs are equal to that of a comparable full shopper. Decisions made in a "hot" state, different than our normal state, will result in less satisfaction in the future.

How emotions affect our finances

If emotions can bring out the darker sides of people and change the course of history, imagine how much impact they can have on your day-to-day life, including your finances. Examining how emotions influence your thoughts and actions can better equip you to make emotionally well-grounded financial decisions. Here is a few emotion that affects our financial decisions:

Feeling sad?

Shopping is called retail therapy for a reason. Buying stuff can make us feel better and chase away the blues, at least temporarily. The problem's when the credit card bills arrive.

Sadness increases the amount of money we're willing to spend and makes us impatient, Harvard University researcher Jennifer Lerner and her colleagues found. When we're sad, we're more likely to give up a larger future benefit to have a smaller benefit right now. That's the exact opposite of the ability to delay gratification, which is what we need to save money and build wealth.

Be aware when you're sad that what you need isn't more stuff. Exercise, time spent outdoors, or hanging out with a comforting friend will provide more relief. If you can't shake your sadness, you may be suffering from depression and should seek treatment.

When you're angry

Anger is a very powerful emotion that causes us to make impulsive financial decisions in the heat of the moment, even the great Warren Buffet fell prey to this emotion. In 1962, Warren Buffet and Seabury Stanton, the CEO of Berkshire Hathaway at the time, had a gentleman's agreement on an offer price at which Berkshire shares would be repurchased from Buffet. However, when Buffet received the offer, he noticed that the CEO's offer price was lower than they had previously agreed. Buffet took this as a personal insult and bought a controlling share in the company just so he could have the pleasure of firing the CEO.

Although this might have given Buffet satisfaction at the time, he ended up wasting precious time and resources reforming a company that was in terminal decline, instead of allocating his funds into more profitable ventures; Mr. Buffet himself labeled this – ***The worst investment he ever made***. Anger causes us to make impulsive financial decisions, by making us blind to the downside of our actions in the heat of the moment.

How to reframe it

What is required to prevent angry financial decisions is an objective third party, in the form of a financial adviser or a friend that can give you the distance you need to put aside your anger and make more rational choices.

I would also advise that, as much as possible, we refrain from making important financial decisions in the heat of the moment. Taking a step back and a few deep breaths to clear your mind off anger will help you minimize impulsive decisions that you will most likely regret in the future.

If you're scared

Anxiety stems from a place of fearful uncertainty, usually characterized by a sense of worry and general unease when thinking about an uncertain outcome. How anxiety affects our financial decisions depends on what the underlying cause of anxiety is i.e. what exactly we're fearful of.

Fear of becoming a bag lady can induce us to save. Fear of leaving our loved ones impoverished can lead us to buy life insurance.

It has the exact opposite effect of anger, making us exaggerate risks rather than discount them. Fear also causes us to second-guess ourselves, making us abandon a plan of action if it goes even slightly off course. For example, you may bail out of a stock when the market hits bottom (and miss the subsequent rebound).

Once again, we can benefit from an experienced guide, such as a financial planner, to discuss our fears and help us stay the course.

How to Reframe It

The problem when dealing with anxiety is that it's quite difficult to "think" your way to a solution; anxiety will have you endlessly playing out different worst-case scenarios in your head. You can only minimize anxiety's influence on your financial decisions when the whirlwind of thoughts is minimized and controlled.

Here are a few steps to help you do just that:

Separate Fact and Fiction

An important first step to curtailing anxiety is sorting out your thoughts by separating what is a **fact** from **fiction**. For instance, your office has announced that it will be downsizing (**Fact**). You think you will be fired and never be able to find another job and end up losing your family (**Fiction**). Although this sorting process is easier said than done, making this separation is an important starting point.

Devise helpful plans

After identifying the Facts and Fiction, the next step is to use the Facts to devise concrete plans that will ease your anxiety.

Speak to an advisor

It is advisable to speak to an experienced guide, like a financial advisor or knowledgeable trusted friend, who can help you develop your plans and whom you can discuss your financial fears with. Getting an outside perspective on the things you're anxious about will help you minimize fearful thinking and objectively weigh up the risks and rewards of each financial decision you have to make. For instance, I could be benefitting from bitcoin's tremendous growth today if I had spoken to a crypto-currency advisor to weigh up the pros and cons of the bitcoin investment years back.

Work with your body

Bodily activities such as regular exercise and conscious breathing can significantly help you control anxious thinking. Practicing conscious breathing by taking 5 deep breaths in through your nose and out through your mouth will slow your heart rate, calm your mind and help you reduce anxiety.

Jealousy

So, a friend of yours just put a down payment on a house while you're still living with your parents and you're feeling a little...jealous. According to

Amy Jo Lauber, president of Lauber Financial Planning, this is a perfectly normal reaction. “Humans are social creatures in a constant state of comparison,” she says.

However, it is important that we don’t become obsessed with keeping up appearances and overly concerned with what others are doing, which are two prevalent problems in the world today. If you’re unable to curb jealously, likely, you’ll continuously spend above your means and end up in some form of debt as a result.

How to reframe it

Turn your jealousy into an opportunity for growth by using it to instigate a period of self-examination about your finances. Drake once said “Jealousy is just loved and hate at the same time” – you **love** what the person has, but you **hate** that you’re not the one that has it. So, during your self-examination, think:

“What is one thing that I want and I don’t have?”

“What is missing in my life right now?”

Is it a vacation?

A new car?

The key is to let your jealousy fuel your desire to work **harder** and make **smarter** money decisions — like forgoing expensive meals out a few nights a week or saving the money you spend on premium TV channels you never actually watch — for you to be able to afford the things you covet.

Feeling guilty?

Guilt is what we feel when we violate our internal standards. If we value our family but spend too much time working, we feel guilty—and may try to make up for that with expensive presents or dinners out.

People who are more prone to guilt are also more prone to altruism. In the best-case scenario, altruism can lead us to share our abundance with others through charitable contributions. In the worst case, we can spend the money we need for ourselves on others.

Here is where setting limits can help. We can keep ourselves from going overboard by creating budgets for spending that can't be influenced by guilt, such as holiday presents.

Excitement

The ever-present feeling of stress in today's world has left humans yearning for something, anything, to celebrate and be excited about. The cause of excitement could be anything ranging from a wedding to the purchase of a new car/house. However, excitement could have seriously harmful effects on our finances and I'll explain how with a story:

Some time ago, a friend called Manuel was excited about his first self-financed trip to Nigeria. He was hell-bent on absorbing as much of Nigeria as he could during his 3-week holiday and set a £500 (₦236,000) budget to do just that. When he arrived in Lagos, he went everywhere; from seminars and meetings on the Mainland to parties and the Migos concert on the Island. It was a well-rounded visit.

When he returned to England and was able to settle down with his bank statement, he found out that he had gone over his budget by £500, far more than he anticipated or had previously planned for. You see excitement tends to make us spend more money than we would under normal circumstances. Although there's nothing wrong with spending money to celebrate, we mustn't get carried away with our spending, or we could end up regretting our decisions later on when we're sober and financially depleted. Unfortunately, this is one of most reasons for which people spend.

How to reframe it

If you want to minimize bad financial decisions when you're excited, what you need is a spending limit to prevent you from going overboard. Your spending limit should be an amount that you can afford and not regret what you spent at a future date. Having a financial limit in mind serves as a reference point every time you consider spending money.

You can also take the spending limit strategy to another level by creating a separate account, which is what my friend did. He took **two key steps** to ensure that he never overspent due to excitement again:

He opened a separate account called "rocks account", which contains ALL the money he's allowed to spend for any particular cause of excitement (like a trip or a party). This account acts as a great way to limit overspending because once money in that account is finished, excitement spending is over.

He also designed a strict personal budget and uses it to do a monthly financial review which ensures that he's on top of his finances at all times.

When you're thankful

Gratitude isn't just a pleasant emotion. Feeling thankful also "reduces excessive economic impatience," according to another study. It helps offset our tendency to discount the value of future rewards—in other words, it helps us delay gratification.

So next time you're struck by the urge to spend money or dip into your savings, take a moment and list at least 10 things that make you feel grateful. You may well decide that you have more than enough.

Chapter 2

MITIGATING EMOTIONAL IMPACTS ON FINANCIAL DECISIONS

This is not to say that emotional influences automatically lead to poor decisions. In fact, people with very low levels of emotion are less likely to conform to social norms and might experience harm as a result. Also, a lack of fear can lead to excessively risky choices.

Being self-aware of how emotions influence your decisions will enable you to assess if the influence is positive or negative and adjust appropriately. As a start, we can ask questions such as: Are the feelings I'm experiencing helpful or harmful? Are they based on facts? Are there other emotions that would be more beneficial?

Emotions are one aspect of effective decision making and taking the time to consider their impact can lead to more effective decisions.

The Impact Of Emotions On Financial Decisions

A study performed by Nobel Prize-winning psychologist Daniel Kahneman showed that we make financial decisions based 90% on emotion and only 10% on logic. But how does that play out in real life?

Financial therapist and wealth counselor Marilyn Wechter points to philanthropy as an example of how feelings encourage us to act. "Philanthropy isn't just a strategy to reduce your tax liability, but a wonderful thing to do that's usually motivated by emotion," she said.

Alan Wolberg, manager of wealth planning at City National Bank, agreed: "Most clients don't take action to prevent or redirect that tax loss unless you get them emotionally involved with helping their community."

Research indicates that the act of giving elicits happiness in the benefactor, even if it requires some sacrifice on their part. A person who donates money to charity often does so with the understanding that it will benefit their community in meaningful ways, thus making them feel good about the gift.

Of course, emotions can also cause irrational behavior as well. They can make you hold onto "residual self-images" — views you hold of yourself as you used to be instead of who you are now — and drive faulty financial decisions based on those perceptions.

Wolberg encounters this phenomenon with his clients too. "They have a residual self-image of what they were when they first started out," he noted. "This means that people tend to manage their wealth using old habits rather than adapting to their changed higher net worth circumstances."

Tips To Help You Make Better Financial Decisions

Understand that your emotions can affect your judgment

A 2007 *Academy of Management Journal* study showed that people who could identify the emotions they were feeling were able to make better decisions, in part due to a greater ability to control any biases caused by those feelings.

Wechter calls this "making conscious the unconscious" — bringing your emotions and beliefs to the front of your mind so you can better understand their influence on you.

"Emotions are neither good nor bad," she explained. "The goal isn't to be emotionless, but to understand the emotions that are driving your decisions. Be clear about where your feelings are coming from, so you can look at things as realistically as possible."

Still, emotions are temporary — while the impact of your financial decisions can be permanent or difficult to change. That's why awareness and moderation of your emotions is crucial when it comes to these choices.

Focus on facts rather than your feelings

Simply concentrating on the facts can often be enough to shake the hold your emotions have on your behavior.

In some cases, it's just a matter of breaking down the numbers in your financial plan to prove that it makes sense. Wolberg often works with clients who hesitate to take advantage of tax-advantaged wealth transfer opportunities because they worry that they'll need the money in the future.

"I try to get clients to objectively understand how they actually *are*, not how they *feel* they are," he remarked. "If I can prove to them that they have more than enough money to fulfill all of their lifestyle needs forever, that opens up an opportunity to do other prudent things with regards to risk management, wealth transfer and philanthropic planning. It gets emotions out of the way."

If you think your emotions might be affecting your ability to think rationally about a situation, you might want to take a page out of Wolberg's book and focus on the facts at hand. Writing down everything you know to be true about the situation can keep these details top of mind and help you review the scenario with more clarity. Or, you can talk things over with someone you trust to bring you an outside perspective.

Identify your money scripts

While growing up, you likely learned lessons about money and wealth from your parents, other family members, important life events, and society that formed your basic assumptions about finances. Some financial psychologists refer to these lessons as "money scripts."

No matter how hard you try, some situations make it nearly impossible to separate feelings from facts. If you feel that your emotions are clouding your judgment, it's important to recognize what triggers them.

You don't have to let your emotions run your financial life. By understanding the money scripts that drive your behavior, you can replace unhelpful thoughts and habits with better ones.

So where do you begin? First, create an internal money dialogue by asking yourself questions and answering them truthfully in a notebook or on a piece of paper.

Some questions to help you get started include:

- How do you use money today and what role does it play in your life?
- What was your earliest memory about money?
- What did you learn about money from your parents? Other family members?

- What was your socioeconomic status growing up and how did you feel about it?
- What is your biggest financial fear?
- Why do certain emotions or behaviors show up when money is involved?
- What core values do you believe in? Are your financial habits supporting those values?
- Are the feelings I'm experiencing helpful or harmful?
- Are they based on facts?
- Are there other emotions that would be more beneficial?

Change starts with awareness. When you understand the roots of your behaviors, you can begin to relearn them — or replace them entirely.

Learn About Your Relationship With Money To Learn About Yourself

Even though wealth planning is driven by facts and numbers, it's also important to take into account your feelings and beliefs about money. Money is intensely personal — people dedicate so much of their lives to earning it, and nearly everything they do requires it in some shape or form — and humans are emotional beings by nature.

As you grow your wealth, it's important to work with a financial advisor who can dissuade you from making detrimental, emotionally driven decisions. And in some cases, additional work with a therapist specializing in money issues can help you understand why certain behaviors show up in the first place.

"How we deal with money is not unlike how we deal with love, power and other things," reflected Wechter. "How we use money says a lot about us, so it's worth understanding.

Chapter 3

CONTROLLING YOUR EMOTIONS

Powerful emotions can feel like you're on a runaway horse. Emotional self-regulation helps you take back the reins.

Emotions are a natural and wonderful part of life. They color our world, help guide us through life, and give us insight into our inner thought processes.

But what happens when our emotions feel like they're controlling us instead of the other way around?

Overwhelming emotions can result in emotional blow-outs, damaged relationships, and poor life decisions. Although it takes some practice, anyone can learn to better control their emotions and use them in more productive ways.

Decide what you want from life

The average person makes 35,000 decisions per day.

Whether you're ordering dinner, picking a movie, or deciding on your ideal relationship, trying to sort through the plethora of choices is overwhelming. And every decision demands a fraction of your mental energy.

It's no wonder why life's biggest decisions feel so exhausting. Questions like, "What do I want to do with my life," "Who do I want to be," and "Where should I live" demand a significant amount of mental energy.

If you're not intentional about figuring out what you want in life, it's easy to fall into survival mode. You become lost, focusing only on what's in front of you, which leads to frustration and disillusionment.

Often, if you don't know what you want, you can become bored and restless with what you're doing, even if you used to love it. Over time this can increase stress, depression, anxiety and can make you feel like you don't have any control over your life.

Figuring out what you want in life is important because it gives you purpose, can influence your career path, and makes life worth living.

We're here to help you decide what you want in life and who you want to be.

A few questions to help you understand what you want in life

The world can feel overwhelming. There are so many paths available to you that indecision is totally normal. But analysis paralysis isn't the answer. You have to overcome your fears and try new things. In the end, chasing after what you want will transform you into the best version of yourself.

Below are some important questions to determine where you want to go in life:

1. What makes you happy?

How do you want to live? Everyone wants to be happy, but happiness isn't just feeling joyful. It's also feeling needed, having a purpose, and maintaining that happiness amid uncertainty.

Both external and internal factors impact our happiness. The former can include our neighborhood or country, while the latter can include our skill sets and self-esteem.

Making a list of everything that makes you happy is a good place to start.

2. What are your needs?

Sometimes, our wants and needs go hand in hand. Other times, what we need isn't what we want.

Ask yourself which of your needs are fulfilled and which aren't. This could refer to your emotional, financial, or physical needs. Keeping a journal can help you get to know yourself, which will help you decide what to do next.

3. What are your personal values?

Remember that values aren't the same as goals. Your core values are principles that guide you through life. They can be anything from patience, honesty, integrity, loyalty, family, and freedom. Most of us prefer to live by our values and identifying your own will help you figure out what you want.

4. What gives you purpose?

Everyone is passionate about something. Maybe it's cooking, looking after family members, or working with animals. When we do what fulfills us, that infectious energy positively impacts others, too.

5. What activities put you in a flow state?

"Flow" refers to the joy we feel when we're right where we're meant to be. It means we're so focused on what we're doing we lose track of time. We're performing at our best and problem-solving more efficiently.

Is there an activity that causes you to feel this way? Pay attention and make a note: what are you usually doing when you're in a flow state?

6. What would you do if there were no limits?

When times are tough, we stop ourselves from dreaming because we feel limited by external factors, like money or vacation days. But don't be afraid to think big. If these limits weren't a factor, what would you do? If there's something you want, you can make a plan to obtain it.

7. Who do you admire or get jealous of?

Do you look up to someone? This person could be an activist, artist, teacher, doctor, or a parent — anyone who leads by example. Think about whether you want to emulate this person.

You should also pay attention to unpleasant feelings like jealousy. Maybe you know someone who's just landed a dream job or went on an amazing trip. Ask yourself why you're jealous.

Self-awareness will help you understand why you feel the way you do.

8. How do you envision the patterns of your life?

Each area of our lives impacts one another, like our health, confidence, resilience, career, and family. Deciding what kind of life you want will determine how it will unfold. Our underlying desire is to change the direction we're walking.

Life is dynamic. And although we can't always control how things go, recognizing this domino effect can give us clarity and help set priorities.

9. What don't you want?

Knowing what to avoid can empower you to make better decisions. Think about what drains you mentally and emotionally, makes you sad, or causes pain.

You can set clear goals — career goals, wellness goals, financial goals — to avoid these pitfalls.

10. What are your greatest accomplishments in life?

Maybe you've won a soccer championship or graduated with honors in mathematics. Did you feel pride in your abilities after this happened? Is there a way for you to live a life that repeats those feelings?

11. Are you willing to work hard?

Victories, both large and small, require hard work. Nothing is just going to fall into your lap. Resilience, venturing outside your comfort zone and learning as much as you can open even more doors for you.

Develop your emotional intelligence

What is emotional intelligence or EQ?

Emotional intelligence (otherwise known as emotional quotient or EQ) is the ability to understand, use, and manage your own emotions in positive ways to relieve stress, communicate effectively, empathize with others, overcome challenges and defuse conflict. Emotional intelligence helps you build stronger relationships, succeed at school and work, and achieve your career and personal goals. It can also help you to connect with your feelings, turn intention into action, and make informed decisions about what matters most to you.

Emotional intelligence is commonly defined by four attributes:

1. **Self-management** – You're able to control impulsive feelings and behaviors, manage your emotions in healthy ways, take initiative, follow through on commitments, and adapt to changing circumstances.
2. **Self-awareness** – You recognize your own emotions and how they affect your thoughts and behavior. You know your strengths and weaknesses, and have self-confidence.

3. **Social awareness** – You have empathy. You can understand the emotions, needs, and concerns of other people, pick up on emotional cues, feel comfortable socially, and recognize the power dynamics in a group or organization.

4. **Relationship management** – You know how to develop and maintain good relationships, communicate clearly, inspire and influence others, work well in a team, and manage conflict.

Why is emotional intelligence so important?

As we know, it's not the smartest people who are the most successful or the most fulfilled in life. You probably know people who are academically brilliant and yet are socially inept and unsuccessful at work or in their personal relationships. Intellectual ability or your intelligence quotient (IQ) isn't enough on its own to achieve success in life. Yes, your IQ can help you get into college, but it's your EQ that will help you manage the stress and emotions when facing your final exams. IQ and EQ exist in tandem and are most effective when they build off one another.

Emotional intelligence affects:

Your performance at school or work. High emotional intelligence can help you navigate the social complexities of the workplace, lead and motivate others, and `excel in your career. In fact, when it comes to gauging important job candidates, many companies now rate emotional intelligence as important as technical ability and employ EQ testing before hiring.

Your physical health. If you're unable to manage your emotions, you are probably not managing your stress either. This can lead to serious health problems. Uncontrolled stress raises blood pressure, suppresses the immune system, increases the risk of heart attacks and strokes, contributes to infertility, and speeds up the aging process. The first step to improving emotional intelligence is to learn how to manage stress.

Your mental health. Uncontrolled emotions and stress can also impact your mental health, making you vulnerable to anxiety and depression. If you are unable to understand, get comfortable with, or manage your emotions, you'll also struggle to form strong relationships. This in turn can leave you feeling lonely and isolated and further exacerbate any mental health problems.

Your relationships. By understanding your emotions and how to control them, you're better able to express how you feel and understand how others are feeling. This allows you to communicate more effectively and forge stronger relationships, both at work and in your personal life.

Your social intelligence. Being in tune with your emotions serves a social purpose, connecting you to other people and the world around you. Social intelligence enables you to recognize friend from foe, measure another person's interest in you, reduce stress, balance your nervous system through social communication, and feel loved and happy.

Building emotional intelligence: Four key skills to increasing your EQ

The skills that make up emotional intelligence can be learned at any time. However, it's important to remember that there is a difference between simply learning about EQ and applying that knowledge to your life. Just because you know you should do something doesn't mean you will—especially when you become overwhelmed by stress, which can override your best intentions. In order to permanently change behavior in ways that stand up under pressure, you need to learn how to overcome stress in the moment, and in your relationships, in order to remain emotionally aware.

The key skills for building your EQ and improving your ability to manage emotions and connect with others are:

1. Self-management
2. Self-awareness
3. Social awareness
4. Relationship management

Self-management

In order for you to engage your EQ, you must be able to use your emotions to make constructive decisions about your behavior. When you become overly stressed, you can lose control of your emotions and the ability to act thoughtfully and appropriately.

Think about a time when stress has overwhelmed you. Was it easy to think clearly or make a rational decision? Probably not. When you become overly stressed, your ability to both think clearly and accurately assess your emotions and other people's becomes compromised.

Emotions are important pieces of information that tell you about yourself and others, but in the face of stress that takes us out of our comfort zone, we can become overwhelmed and lose control of ourselves. With the ability to manage stress and stay emotionally present, you can learn to receive upsetting information without letting it override your thoughts and self-control. You'll be able to make choices that allow you to control impulsive feelings and behaviors, manage your emotions in healthy ways, take initiative, follow through on commitments, and adapt to changing circumstances.

Self-awareness

Managing stress is just the first step to building emotional intelligence. The science of attachment indicates that your current emotional experience is likely a reflection of your early life experience. Your ability to manage core feelings such as anger, sadness, fear, and joy often depends on the quality and consistency of your early life emotional experiences. If your primary caretaker as an infant understood and valued your emotions, it's likely your emotions have become valuable assets in adult life. But, if your emotional experiences as an infant were confusing, threatening or painful, it's likely you've tried to distance yourself from your emotions.

But being able to connect to your emotions—having a moment-to-moment connection with your changing emotional experience—is the key to understanding how emotion influences your thoughts and actions.

Do you experience feelings that flow, encountering one emotion after another as your experiences change from moment to moment?

Are your emotions accompanied by physical sensations that you experience in places like your stomach, throat, or chest?

Do you experience individual feelings and emotions, such as anger, sadness, fear, and joy, each of which is evident in subtle facial expressions?

Can you experience intense feelings that are strong enough to capture both your attention and that of others?

Do you pay attention to your emotions? Do they factor into your decision making?

If any of these experiences are unfamiliar, you may have "turned down" or "turned off" your emotions. In order to build EQ—and become emotionally healthy—you must reconnect to your core emotions, accept them, and become comfortable with them. You can achieve this through the practice of mindfulness.

Mindfulness is the practice of purposely focusing your attention on the present moment—and without judgment. The cultivation of mindfulness has roots in Buddhism, but most religions include some type of similar prayer or meditation technique. Mindfulness helps shift your preoccupation with thought toward an appreciation of the moment, your physical and emotional sensations, and brings a larger perspective on life. Mindfulness calms and focuses you, making you more self-aware in the process.

Developing emotional awareness

Social awareness

Social awareness enables you to recognize and interpret the mainly nonverbal cues others are constantly using to communicate with you. These cues let you know how others are really feeling, how their emotional state is changing from moment to moment, and what's truly important to them.

When groups of people send out similar nonverbal cues, you're able to read and understand the power dynamics and shared emotional experiences of the group. In short, you're empathetic and socially comfortable.

Mindfulness is an ally to emotional and social awareness

To build social awareness, you need to recognize the importance of mindfulness in the social process. After all, you can't pick up on subtle nonverbal cues when you're in your own head, thinking about other things, or simply zoning out on your phone. Social awareness requires your presence in the moment. While many of us pride ourselves on an ability to multitask, this means that you'll miss the subtle emotional shifts taking place in other people that help you fully understand them.

You are actually more likely to further your social goals by setting other thoughts aside and focusing on the interaction itself.

Following the flow of another person's emotional responses is a give-and-take process that requires you to also pay attention to the changes in your own emotional experience.

Paying attention to others doesn't diminish your own self-awareness. By investing the time and effort to really pay attention to others, you'll actually gain insight into your own emotional state as well as your values and beliefs. For example, if you feel discomfort hearing others express certain views, you'll have learned something important about yourself.

Relationship management

Working well with others is a process that begins with emotional awareness and your ability to recognize and understand what other people are experiencing. Once emotional awareness is in play, you can effectively develop additional social/emotional skills that will make your relationships more effective, fruitful, and fulfilling.

Become aware of how effectively you use nonverbal communication. It's impossible to avoid sending nonverbal messages to others about what you think and feel. The many muscles in the face, especially those around the eyes, nose, mouth and forehead, help you to wordlessly convey your own emotions as well as read other peoples' emotional intent. The emotional part of your brain is always on—and even if you ignore its messages—others won't. Recognizing the nonverbal messages that you send to others can play a huge part in improving your relationships.

Use humor and play to relieve stress. Humor, laughter and play are natural antidotes to stress. They lessen your burdens and help you keep things in perspective. Laughter brings your nervous system into balance, reducing stress, calming you down, sharpening your mind and making you more empathic.

Learn to see conflict as an opportunity to grow closer to others. Conflict and disagreements are inevitable in human relationships. Two people can't possibly have the same needs, opinions, and expectations at all times. However, that needn't be a bad thing. Resolving conflict in healthy, constructive ways can strengthen trust between people. When conflict isn't perceived as threatening or punishing, it fosters freedom, creativity, and safety in relationships.

Chapter 4

Why the rich keep getting richer: learn and join them.

I remember reading an article about Ringo Starr, the famed drummer of The Beatles. He said something in the article which got me thinking.

When Ringo was a young lad and just started out in music, all he wanted was to own a nice drum set. He didn't have money and needed to claw and scrape to save enough to buy the nice drum set in order to make music. No one offered to help him out on the purchase.

Now after having achieved fame and fortune, he gets offered free drums all the time from companies. In fact, I'm sure not only can he get free drums; he can get companies to pay him to use their drums.

Ringo found it ironic that when he was young, broke, and needed financial help, no one offered any help to him. But now that he is rich, famous, and can easily afford any drum set in the world, he can get them for free any day of the week.

Now is this fair? Hard to say – it really depends on your perspective. But that is how the world works.

The truth about this is that "**The World Gives More to Those Who Have More**".

No matter how much money you earn, you'll always be poor if you spend more than you make.

However, most rich people don't do those things, and that's part of how they build and maintain their wealth. There's a difference between living a life of careless spending (which will quickly drain even a wealthy person's bank account) and living for long-term financial independence and wealth.

The self-made rich aren't necessarily smarter than anyone else, but they have mastered some important principles that help them get ahead and stay ahead. Most importantly, they treat building wealth as a learnable skill -- and it's one that you can learn, too.

So, if you'd like to join the ranks of the super wealthy, try honing these 11 habits and lifestyle changes and see what financial freedom truly feels like.

Reasons why the rich keep getting richer

There are good reasons why the rich are getting richer. The purpose of this work is not to draw up hate or jealousy of the rich. It's to make you see that there are reasons why it is easier for the rich to gain more coins than the average person. And those reasons have nothing to do with being evil, being a bad person or performing illegal acts as the general population is led to believe. The better part of this is that you too can learn and make them your personal beliefs and everyday habits.

1. The Rich Place Higher Value On Their Time

If you go to work, you expect to get paid for your time and effort. I hope that seems reasonable to all of us, except for a few politicians out there who believe you should be tax heavily on your effort and collect very little for your labor.

If the economy is good, I assume you will take a job only if it pays you at least what you think is a good price on your time. If the job doesn't pay you what you believe you should make, you will probably decide to walk away and look for a new job.

The rich feel the same way except they might place more value on their time. We all work for money accordingly to what we believe is a fair exchange for our time. The rich end up getting more money for hours worked because they believe a higher pay amount is necessary for their time

This makes sense given the rich already have a sizable asset pool. They tend to compare compensation to their asset pool. $100,000 a year might sound good to someone with $25,000 in assets. But if you have

$10 million in assets, $100,000 a year in compensation for working a job doesn't sound as great.

Therefore, the rich will elect to work on something that can produce a higher compensation. Hopefully, this seems logical to you and is one of the reasons why the rich continue to get richer. They place more value on their time.

2. Have a financial growth mindset.

Wealthy people are incredibly creative when it comes to thinking about business and finding different ways of making money. Mega-successful people set themselves apart because they nurture a financial growth mindset, which changes how you view money and helps you focus on seeing profitable opportunities.

This mindset helps successful and wealthy people believe that there are always bigger and better projects to work on and there's always more money to be made. They're open to exploring new ideas. They believe they're always capable of making changes and creating a positive outcome. If you don't believe in yourself, how can anybody else?

In *You Are a Badass at Making Money*, Jen Sincero shares how limiting beliefs get in the way of making the type of money you really want.

Whenever the gurus of the world talk about mindsets, they're talking about your personal beliefs and how they can get in the way of finding success or achieving personal satisfaction.

Before talking about the benefits of cultivating a growth mindset, it helps to start by first defining the opposite situation: a fixed mindset.

A fixed mindset involves a self-imposed limitation -- like what Sincero discusses in terms of personal finance. As Carol Dweck wrote in her book *MindSet: The New Psychology of Success*, "It assumes that our character, intelligence and creative ability are *static* givens which we can't change in any meaningful way".

Also according to Dweck, a growth mindset is "the tendency to believe that you can grow."

Doing battle with an existing fixed mindset

Before you can embrace a growth mindset, you need to be able to admit to yourself if you're currently stuck in a fixed mindset.

For those operating with a fixed mindset, the belief is that effort is not required to succeed because intellect cannot be changed. Those with a fixed mindset truly believe that their existing talent, skills and intelligence alone can lead them to success -- so long as they stay in their lane.

People with a growth mindset believe that going after challenges provides the ability to see failure as part of learning and growth -- instead of it being evidence of unintelligence. This mindset offers permission to experiment, with the understanding that intelligence and skill develop with time and experience. As a result, people operating with a growth mindset give themselves permission to increase their efforts when they believe in something.

To be sure, most people are operating with both mindsets simultaneously -- a different mindset for different aspects of their lives. The key to overcoming limiting beliefs is to first recognize them, then to consciously choose to think a different way.

Acknowledge your weakness.

Staying in your comfort zone makes it hard for growth to happen. Consider this example: Recall a time when you were in school and were dealing with a subject that you struggled with. Perhaps you told people, "I'm just not a science person" after dealing with a string of bad test grades.

If you ever want to get better, you must first stop with the excuses -- they'll keep you exactly where you are.

If you were to instead tell yourself, "I'm currently struggling with science but I know that I could be better with more practice," you're putting yourself in the right direction to get a good grade on your next test (assuming you follow through with that extra practice).

It helps to give yourself a specific reason to get over your limiting mindsets (e.g. "I want to get a better grade on my science tests").

Of course, the process to successfully adopt a growth mindset is a bit more complicated than that -- so let's dig in a bit deeper.

Learn to see challenges as opportunities.

For those with a growth mindset, challenges are seen as an opportunity to grow and learn, rather than just being an obstacle. People with growth mindsets aren't afraid to push themselves outside of their comfort zones -- they embrace the opportunity to learn from however the experience eventually shakes out.

When's the last time you were challenged to do something outside of your comfort zone? Even if it was terrifying to put yourself out there, you'll likely find that it all turned out for the best in the end -- better than if you hadn't taken a chance. Even if you failed.

Learn how to accept failure.

If you learn how to accept challenges and see them as opportunities, you must also learn to accept failure and be willing to take risks. After all, failure is part of growth and fearing failure will ultimately get in the way of doing what's best for your business.

To truly create a growth mindset, you must accept that no matter how hard you try to do something, it won't always turn out the way you'd hoped.

Consider this: If J.K Rowling stopped submitting the Harry Potter series to publishers after her first rejection (or the twelfth rejection before it reached Bloomberry), she wouldn't have been able to sell more than 500 million copies worldwide.

Don't seek approval. Focus on learning.

People with a fixed mindset spend a lot of time worrying about what other people will say about their intelligence and talent. In order to embrace a growth mindset, you must learn how to stop being concerned about what other people think and about getting their approval.

So, focus on your own learning and growth. Instead of spending your precious time thinking about other people, use this time to improve yourself for your own benefit.

Learn how to effectively accept (and use) criticism.

Most people can't accept criticism without getting offended. But, in order to cultivate a growth mindset, you must learn not to take criticism as a negative thing. Instead, accept that criticism is a way to learn and improve.

Smart businesses encourage feedback, ratings and reviews. Whenever they're negative, growth-focused businesses use this information to make improvements.

Focus on the process, not the result

Rather than being too concerned with whether you're achieving the result you desire, focus more on the process of achieving that result. Learn how to enjoy the learning process, and seek out ideas to make improvements as you go.

Create time for daily reflection.

At the end of every day, spend some time thinking about what went well ... and what didn't. If you don't create time to reflect, it's hard to learn.

Creating a routine around reflection can help you to understand how your own actions may be impeding your success, before they become a major issue.

Whether you're an employee at a company or have started your own venture, the ability to move from a fixed mindset to one that's focused on growth is necessary to overcome limiting thoughts. At the end of the day, it's up to *you* to determine what you're capable of -- nobody else can tell you otherwise.

3. Network with other successful people.

Wealthy people understand the importance of surrounding themselves with other successful people. Wealthy people spend time networking with others who are wealthy but also have drive, talent and, most important, the potential to become wildly successful. The rich spend time every month getting to know other like-minded people at conferences, events and gatherings, or just grabbing coffee or a drink with someone interesting.

This is time wisely invested, as it keeps their minds focused on success and helps them meet new people who have fresh and thought-provoking ideas. Doing this also helps wealthy people fill their contact lists with relevant and influential people who can potentially help them (and vice versa).

4. Get outside your comfort zone.

Wealthy people are successful because they have learned that success comes to those who embrace a little discomfort. They understand that the only way to really improve is to push yourself beyond your limits. If you want to become wealthy, you're going to need to fuel your creative spark, come up with unique business ideas and then take the plunge.

Wealth and success don't emerge from the safety of a 9-to-5 job. They come from drawing on your inner strength and going for your big dream. All successful business leaders, visionaries and game-changers have gone beyond their comfort zones in order to achieve the ultimate success. The people who will go down in history had the courage to face their fears and take that first step into the unknown.

Why you need to step out if your comfort zone

Getting stuck in a routine is easy to do. After all, we're creatures of habit. We eat the same breakfast every morning, order the same coffee at Starbucks and get to work at the same time.

But for entrepreneurs, playing it safe could be curtailing business success. When's the last time you stepped out of your comfort zone and took on a new challenge?

Dr. Elizabeth Lombardo, therapist and author of better than perfect says people who regularly seek out fresh experiences tend to be more creative and emotionally resilient than those who remain stuck in routine.

"Breaking your own mold can only make you stronger and more confident to reach higher levels in your professional and personal life," she says.

Innovation, she says, happens when we step outside our comfort zone. Being stagnant in routine often results in plummeting creativity. "In order to be more creative, you have to try new things, see things in a new way, put pieces together in a new manner," she says.

What holds most of us back from stepping out of our comfort zone, however, is fear. "We have such a huge fear of failure in our society," says Lombardo. Any new skill always feels awkward and stressful at first, but the more you do it, the more comfortable it will be. Getting comfortable with being uncomfortable, Lombardo says, is the key to overcoming this fear.

Here's how to step out of your comfort zone:

Do it on a regular basis

In order to get comfortable with being uncomfortable, you need to step out of your comfort zone on a regular basis. "The more comfortable you get with trying new things, the less you're going to avoid it and the more you're going to say yes to new challenges," says Lombardo.

Start small

You don't have to throw your entire routine out the window to step out of your comfort zone. Try taking small steps, like driving a different route to work or even moving your desk to a different location. These can help you to get comfortable with the discomfort that comes from trying something new.

Reinterpret your fear

In order to overcome your fear of trying something new, Lombardo recommends re-framing those feelings of fear as feelings of excitement and opportunity. When viewed in this positive light, those butterflies in your stomach will soon be seen as welcoming rather than something that you seek to avoid.

Look for a challenge

"Doing something that challenges you gives you a whole different outlook and makes you more receptive to change," says Lombardo. When you take on something challenging, you experience an endorphin rush and often feel recharged afterwards.

Focus on the why

Having a mission statement of why you're stepping out of your comfort zone can help you overcome the fear of doing it. Lombardo recommends writing out the benefits of doing the activity, such as "to build courage" or "to become more creative." Looking at the why when you start to get stressed out can help bring down your stress levels and make it easier to accomplish the task.

5. Create multiple income flows.

The more money you have, the easier it is to make more money. And the easiest and fastest way to make more money is to have multiple income streams. That way you always have money coming in and can use the excess income to invest in new income flows. This, in a nutshell, is the primary way the wealthy stay wealthy.

There are two basic forms of income: active income, in which you work for the money you make, and passive income, in which payment isn't directly tied to the number of hours you work. Passive income includes rental property, dividend stocks, index funds, writing a book or creating an app, all of which will bring in a steady flow of income from sales or royalties.

6. Invest.

Rich people make their money work for them. They know that investing is the key to growing their finances. While saving money for a rainy day is important, your investments are going to do the heavy lifting to help you become wealthy.

Saving means putting money into a safe place until you want to retrieve it, but most savings accounts don't yield high interest, so this pile of money basically stays static -- it's not going to grow much beyond what you add. But smart investments will give you healthy returns, which you can then reinvest. When you invest in something, you also accept some amount of risk, so you never want to invest more than you can afford to lose.

7. Take calculated risks.

The rich don't gamble on big financial decisions; they do what they can to mitigate risk. They do their research and analysis, and determine which options best suit their financial needs and business desires. They weigh the pros and cons, and then take calculated risks.

They make financial decisions by asking themselves, "Will this bring me closer to my goal?" They avoid frivolous risks that aren't really going to benefit them, and never take a cavalier attitude when it comes to money.

Entrepreneurship is a game of calculated risk

A lot of people seem to associate entrepreneurship with risk. You will hear friends and family mention the turnover ratio in business, or perhaps share stories of people they know who lost all their money in a failed startup. There are certainly many people who opt to not create a small business or build off their idea because they're afraid of failure.

The risk involved with creating a startup and small business is apparent to many. But, if there is so much risk involved, why do entrepreneurs try? And is it even worth it?

The best way to approach this is by comparing a failed startup with a successful startup. When analyzing a failed start up, we can see patterns that formed: poor planning, failure to analyze the market and a lack of structure are all common traits of failed businesses.

Conversely, successful startups tend to have a lot in common: a clear goal, knowledge of the business and competitors and a strong business ethic.

In both of the scenarios, there is unavoidable risk involved. However, there is a large difference between the two businesses. The failed business took a larger risk by entering the market without a proper strategy. The successful business still had to deal with risk, but the entrepreneur behind the business took calculated risks, which are, in other words, intelligent risks.

Understanding calculated risk.

When you begin to build your new business, you will hear your friends and family mention how businesses can easily fail, especially when first starting out. This is certainly true, but you can put your business in the best position to succeed by minimizing big risks and focusing on calculated risk.

Calculated risk is exactly what it sounds like. If you have a big problem in your business, you will likely have a number of options on how to approach it. Each solution will have its own set of benefits and drawbacks and it is up to you, the entrepreneur, to figure out which is going to help your business the most.

An excellent example of calculated risk is baseball. Each player can get up to bat and go for the home run play. While this works for some, it won't work for most. Instead, players will look for individual hits that will eventually lead to scoring plays. They are taking a risk by going for smaller plays, but there is a smaller chance of them failing to convert. This type of calculated risk will win games. Your business isn't going to be any different. You will have opportunities for "home run" decision, and you should take them when the time is right. However, going for the home run each time a decision needs to be made can set your business up for failure, and having a larger perspective on that is one of the best things you can do. Stay focused, keep your eyes on your goal, and only take a big swing when the time is right. You'll know when the time is right.

8. Focus on self-improvement.

Wealthy people are usually avid readers, but you won't find many mindless beach novels in their bookcases. The wealthy understand the importance of self-education and pushing themselves to become better in all ways. In fact, if you look at the books piled by their beds, you'll mostly find titles on self-improvement.

While 85 percent of rich people read two or more self-improvement books per month, only 11 percent read for entertainment, compared to 79 percent of the poor. And a whopping 94 percent of wealthy people read news publications, compared to 11 percent of non-wealthy people.

9. Never completely retire.

The ultra-rich certainly have enough money to never work another day in their life, but the majority of them keep working, at least to some degree, often well past 70. That doesn't mean they're clocking long days at the office; indeed, they're probably taking their fair share of vacations and enjoying flexible schedules. But many rich people never completely retire. This is not because they can't afford to, but because they enjoy what they do.

Many are entrepreneurs at heart, and the desire to run and grow a business never leaves them. The stability of working and the sense of purpose and fulfillment it gives them is an important part of their overall happiness. Working gives them an ongoing feeling of success and an objective to keep them focused. Not to mention that it keeps the money rolling in!

10. Avoid overspending.

While non-wealthy people daydream about spending money without worry, buying fancy cars, big houses and expensive clothes, the rich understand that the more money you spend, the less you have. The wealthy wouldn't stay wealthy long if they spent excessively. No matter how much money you earn, you'll always be poor if you spend more than you make.

The rich recognize that the less you spend, the more money you have to grow your wealth. Keep in mind that frugality is relative to your income -- a wealthy person may spend much more than someone who is considered middle class. But in relative terms, the rich tend to be thrifty, and they make sure they don't overspend.

11. Take time to reflect.

Many of the self-made wealthy spend time in focused thinking every day. Spending 30 minutes (or more) in a quiet space gives them time to reflect on their life and goals, to think about their health and relationships, consider their career and financial goals, and analyze where they're currently at and where they want to be. Critical thinking time is essential to staying ahead of the market and considering what changes may be coming your way.

This is also time to focus on self-improvement and working through ideas. Some may opt for journaling or writing to help them come up with creative solutions and ideas. Just make sure you're spending your time on productive thinking. Don't waste your mental energy on ruminations or negative thought loops that will make you second guess yourself. The wealthy don't.

Conclusion

Knowledge they say is power. But how powerful are those with the knowledge of almost everything but never get to apply it to the right situation. If after all you've learnt from this book, no action is taken towards bettering your life and that of those around you, then it would have been better you did not read it at all. All I'm saying is that; it's one thing to be ignorant and it's entirely another to know. Action makes the difference. So act now. Take control of your emotions, stop acting rich and start getting rich.

www.ingramcontent.com/pod-product-compliance
Lightning Source LLC
LaVergne TN
LVHW050339160826
845677LV00014B/3684

* 9 7 9 8 8 4 6 4 3 8 7 5 0 *